Ladybird  Readers

Great Trains

Series Editor: Sorrel Pitts
Text adapted by Sorrel Pitts
Illustrated by Martin Sanders

LADYBIRD BOOKS

UK | USA | Canada | Ireland | Australia
India | New Zealand | South Africa

Ladybird Books is part of the Penguin Random House group of companies
whose addresses can be found at global.penguinrandomhouse.com.
www.penguin.co.uk   www.puffin.co.uk   www.ladybird.co.uk

Penguin
Random House
UK

First published 2017
002

Copyright © Ladybird Books Ltd, 2017

Printed in China

A CIP catalogue record for this book is available from the British Library

ISBN: 978-0-241-29808-4

All correspondence to:
Ladybird Books
Penguin Random House Children's
One Embassy Gardens, 8 Viaduct Gardens, London SW11 7BW

Great Trains

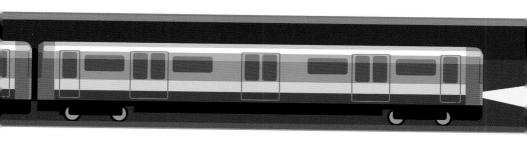

Contents

Picture words

fast train

goods train

new train

old train

passengers

passenger
train

steam train

subway
train

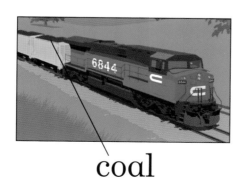

coal

Lots of trains

This is a fast train.

This is a new train.

This is a steam train.

This is a passenger train.

This is a goods train.

Traveling on a train

Do you like traveling? You can take a train!

This train is taking
people on holiday.

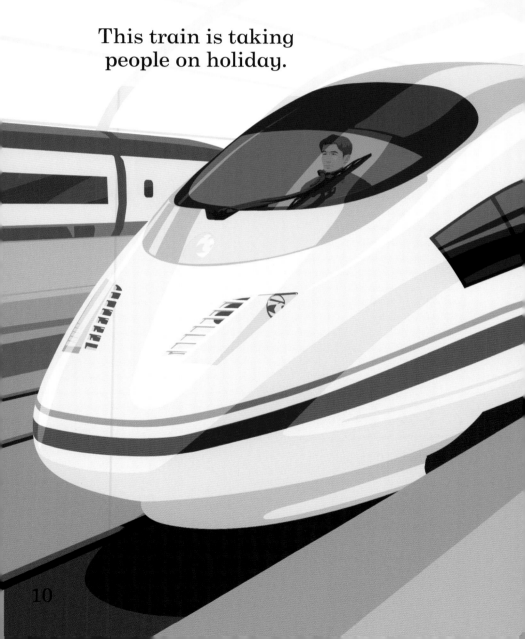

passengers

Trains help people

Look at all these trains.
The trains are taking
people to their jobs.

These trains have got lots of passengers.

13

Goods trains

Trains carry things, too.

goods train

cars

This goods train is carrying cars.

coal

This goods train is carrying coal.

Steam trains

Look at this old steam train.

People love traveling
on these old trains.

steam

This old train is a steam train.

New trains

These new trains look great!

These people are going on holiday.

These people are going to their jobs.

Fast trains

You can travel very fast on this passenger train!

Can you see lots of passengers on the fast train?

fast train

21

Subway trains

These subway trains are taking people under the roads and houses.

Many people go to their jobs on subway trains.

subway train

23

Up and down

Old trains can take
you up . . . and down.

People love going up
and down in trains!

This train is
going down.

down →

This train is going up.

← up

Trains are great!

You can enjoy traveling on . . .

. . . a steam train.

. . . a subway train.

. . . a fast train.

. . . a new train.

Activities

The key below describes the skills practiced in each activity.

Spelling and writing

Reading

Speaking

? Critical thinking

Preparation for the Cambridge Young Learners Exams

1 Match the words to the pictures.

1 steam train

2 passenger train

3 goods train

4 subway train

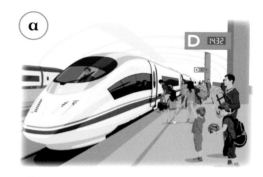

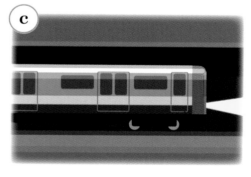

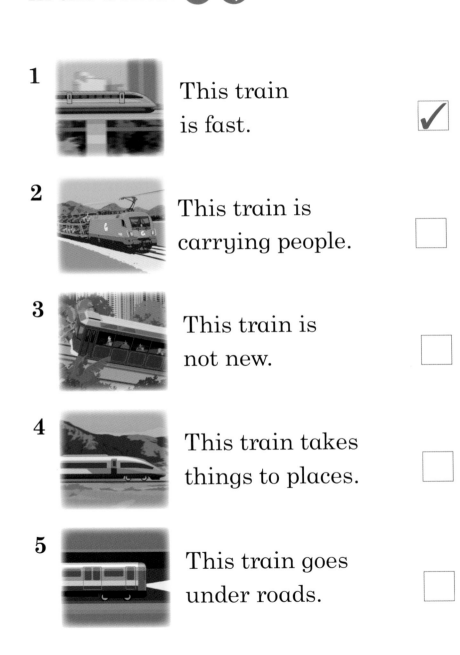

1 This train is fast. ✓

2 This train is carrying people. ☐

3 This train is not new. ☐

4 This train takes things to places. ☐

5 This train goes under roads. ☐

3 Look at the letters. Write the words. 🖊 🌀

1 (a n i t r)

new .... train ....

2 (d o g o s)

.... train

3 (a s p g n s e r e)

.... train

4 (m s e a t)

.... train

5 (y b a w u s)

.... train

4 Choose the correct words and write them on the lines.

take   is taking   travel   traveling

1 Do you like _traveling?_

2 You can _____ a train!

3 This train _____ people on holiday.

4 Passengers _____ to their jobs on a train.

5 **Read the questions.**
Write complete answers.

Trains help people
Look at all these trains.
The trains are taking people to their jobs.
These trains have got lots of passengers.

1 Who do trains help?

Trains help people.

2 Where are these trains taking people?

These trains are taking

.

3 Are they goods trains or passenger trains?

These trains are

.

6 **Put the trains in the correct boxes in the table.** 📖 ✏️

goods train

passenger train

What it does	Which train?
carries cars	goods train
carries people	
takes people to their jobs	
carries coal	

7 Find the words.

a p r c o a l g o o d a p a s s e n g e r s t h i c a r s c h a g o o d s b w y p e o p l e s t i

coal
goods
cars
people
passengers

8 Talk about the two pictures with a friend. How are they different? Use the words in the box. 🗨

passenger   coal   cars
jobs   new   old   goods

a

b

There are passenger trains in picture a.

There are goods trains in picture b.

9 **Circle the correct words.**

1 People love traveling on
goods trains. / steam trains.

2 Steam trains are **old. / new.**

3 People go to their jobs on
passenger trains. / steam trains.

4 **Goods trains / Passenger trains**
take people on holiday.

5 Steam trains are **fast. / slow.**

10 Look at the pictures. Put a 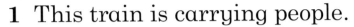 in the correct boxes. 📖

1 This train is carrying people.

2 This train is carrying cars.

3 This train goes fast!

11 Do the crossword.

Down

1 This train carries things and not people.

3 Some people travel to work on passenger . . .

Across

2 Some goods trains carry this.

4 People enjoy traveling on old . . . trains.

5 Some trains travel very . . .

12 Write *This* or *These*.

1 _____These_____ new trains look great!

2 _____ people are going
on holiday.

3 _____ passenger train can
travel very fast!

4 _____ train is new.

13 **Read the text. Choose the correct words, and write them next to 1—5.**

> **1** train   trains   old trains
>
> **2** goods   steam   passenger
>
> **3** Goods   Steam   Subway
>
> **4** under   down   on holiday

People enjoy traveling on fast

[1] _____trains_____. You can travel very

fast on some [2] _____ trains.

[3] _____ trains take people

under the roads and houses. Some old

trains take people up and

[4] _____.

14 **Read the questions. Write answers using words in the box.** 📖 ✏️

> Goods trains   Passenger trains
> Subway trains

1 Which trains carry passengers?

Passenger trains
carry passengers.

2 Which trains carry coal?

_____ carry coal.

3 Which trains take people to work under the roads and houses?

_____ go under the roads and houses.

15 **Ask and answer questions about the picture with a friend.** ●

Trains are great!
You can enjoy traveling on . . .

. . . a steam train.

. . . a fast train.

. . . a subway train.

. . . a new train.

26

27

1 *Which train is your favorite?*

My favorite train is a fast train.

2 Which train is old?

3 Which train goes under the roads?

4 Which train takes people on holiday?

16 **Circle the correct pictures.**

1 Which train travels in the city?

a   b

2 Which train carries goods?

a   b

3 Which train takes people up and down?

a   b

4 Which people are going on holiday?

a   b

17 Write *on*, *under*, or *up*.

1 A subway train takes people

  under the roads.

2 People love going ....
and down on trains.

3 Many people go to their jobs
  .... passenger trains.

4 You can travel very fast
  .... a passenger train.

5 Steam trains do not go
  .... the roads and houses.

18 Write the missing letters.

1

t   s   f

f ast train

2

z   w   s

good_____ train

3

s   a   o

_____ team train

4

dr   pa   te

_____ ssenger train

19 **Draw a picture of a train.**
Answer the questions. 📖 ✏️ ❓

1 What color is your train?
My train is

....

2 What does your train carry?
My train carries

....

3 Where does it travel?
My train travels

....

Level 2

Ladybird ⬤ Readers — Level 2 — **The Gingerbread Man**
978-0-241-25442-4 ☐

Ladybird ⬤ Readers — Level 2 — **Sly Fox and Red Hen**
978-0-241-25443-1 ☐

Ladybird ⬤ Readers — Level 2 — **The Monster Next Door**
978-0-241-25444-8 ☐

Ladybird ⬤ Readers — Level 2 — **Wild Animals**
978-0-241-25445-5 ☐

Ladybird ⬤ Readers — Level 2 — **Little Red Riding Hood**
978-0-241-25446-2 ☐

Ladybird ⬤ Readers — Level 2 — **Dinosaurs**
978-0-241-25447-9 ☐

Ladybird ⬤ Readers — Level 2 — **Topsy and Tim The Big Race**
978-0-241-25448-6 ☐

Ladybird ⬤ Readers — Level 2 — **Goes to the Treehouse**
978-0-241-25449-3 ☐

Ladybird ⬤ Readers — Level 2 — **Sports Day**
978-0-241-26222-1 ☐

Ladybird ⬤ Readers — Level 2 — **Going on a Picnic**
978-0-241-26221-4 ☐

Ladybird ⬤ Readers — Level 2 — **Peter Rabbit and the Angry Owl**
978-0-241-28369-1 ☐

Ladybird ⬤ Readers — Level 2 — **Superhero Max**
978-0-241-28368-4 ☐

Ladybird ⬤ Readers — Level 2 — **We Can Help!**
978-0-241-28367-7 ☐

Ladybird ⬤ Readers — Level 2 — **Daddy Pig's New Van**
978-0-241-28371-4 ☐

Ladybird ⬤ Readers — Level 2 — **School Trip**
978-0-241-28372-1 ☐

Ladybird ⬤ Readers — Level 2 — **The Peter Rabbit Club**
978-0-241-29811-4 ☐

Ladybird ⬤ Readers — Level 2 — **Daddy Pig's Office**
978-0-241-29814-5 ☐

Ladybird ⬤ Readers — Level 2 — **Spring is Here!**
978-0-241-29809-1 ☐

Ladybird ⬤ Readers — Level 2 — **Great Trains**
978-0-241-29808-4 ☐

Ladybird ⬤ Readers — Level 2 — **Hungry Animals**
978-0-241-29844-2 ☐

Now you're ready for Level 3!